Contents

Words appearing in the text in bold, **like this**, are explained in the Glossary.

What was the Holocaust?

In ancient times, the word **Holocaust** meant 'an offering to the gods that was completely burnt away'. By medieval times it was used to mean 'a huge destruction or sacrifice'. From 1700 it was used to talk about the murder of large numbers of people. It is now mostly used to describe the deliberate attempt by the **Nazi** government of Germany to destroy all the **Jewish** people in their power. It was first used in this way in the 1950s.

When did the Holocaust take place?

The Holocaust happened during the Second World War, which lasted from 1939 to 1945. However, Jewish people were persecuted and killed from the moment the Nazis came to power in 1933. The war helped the Nazis to cover up and excuse their move to mass killing.

Historians have tried hard to work out how many people died in the Holocaust. Their work suggests that between 5.1 and 5.8 million were murdered. The scale of the killing was such that a new word was invented to describe it – 'genocide'. Rafael Lemkin, a Jewish lawyer living in the USA, first used this word in 1943 to describe the wiping out of a whole **race**, that is, a group of people with the same **ancestors**. While 'the Holocaust' mostly refers to the Nazi killings, 'genocide' is used to describe any attempt to murder all members of a racial group.

Survivors

In many cases only one or two members of a family survived the Holocaust. In this photograph of the Zylberberg family, only the baby on the right, Perec, survived. His sister, Esther, who was born after the photo was taken, also survived. Another survivor, Norbert Wollheim, said:

> 'All the others who had gone with me to **Auschwitz** or had been taken there at other times, would never return. My wife, my child, my parents and about 70 other relations: uncles, aunts, cousins, all gone.'

Prelude to the Holocaust

Jane Shuter

www.heinemann.co.uk/library
Visit our website to find out more information about **Heinemann Library** books.

To order:
 Phone 44 (0) 1865 888066
 Send a fax to 44 (0) 1865 314091
 Visit the Heinemann Bookshop at www.heinemann.co.uk/library to browse our catalogue and order online.

First published in Great Britain by Heinemann Library, Halley Court, Jordan Hill, Oxford OX2 8EJ, part of Harcourt Education. Heinemann is a registered trademark of Harcourt Education Ltd.

Editorial: Andrew Farrow and Georga Godwin
Design: Joanna Sapwell and Tinstar Design (www.tinstar.co.uk)
Illustrations: Martin Griffin
Picture Research: Maria Joannou and Thelma Gilbert
Production: Viv Hichens

Originated by Ambassador Litho Ltd
Printed in Hong Kong by Wing King Tong

ISBN 0 431 15360 4 (hardback)
06 05 04 03 02
10 9 8 7 6 5 4 3 2 1

ISBN 0 431 15365 5 (paperback)
07 06 05 04 03
10 9 8 7 6 5 4 3 2 1

British Library Cataloguing in Publication Data
Shuter, Jane
The Holocaust: Prelude to the Holocaust
940.5'318
A full catalogue record for this book is available from the British Library.

Acknowledgements
The Publishers would like to thank the following for permission to reproduce photographs: AKG pp. **14**, **47**; Anne Frank Stichting p. **18**; Associated Press pp. **46**, **49**; Auschwitz-Birkenau State Museum pp. **15**, **39**; Bildarchiv Preussisher Kulturbesitz pp. **19**, **26**, **27**, **33**, **40**; Bundesarchive p. **28**; Corbis p. **9**; Emma Robertson & Magnet Harlequin pp. **5** (top), **5** (bottom), **37**; Hessisches Hauptstaatsarchiv in Wiesbaden p. **35**; Hulton Archive p. **23**, **45**; Imperial War Museum p. **32**; Jewish Chronicle p. **48**; Kurt Fuchel p. **49**; Magnum p. **43**; Mary Evans picture library pp. **11**, **12**; Robert Hunt Library (& Mary Evans Reserve) p. **17**; Rudolf Vrba p. **41**; Sterling Memorial Library, Yale University p. **13**; Tomi Ungerer & Diogense Verlag AG Zurich p. **31**; Ullstein Bild p. **30**; USHMM pp. **6**, **7**, **13**, **16**, **20**, **24**, **29**, **44**; Yad Vashem p. **36**, **38**, **42**.

Cover photograph of Adolf Hitler surveying a mass gathering of Nazis, reproduced with permission of Popperfoto.

The publishers would like to thank Jonathan Gorsky of the Council of Christians and Jews for his assistance in the preparation of this book.

Every effort has been made to contact copyright holders of any material reproduced in this book. Any omissions will be rectified in subsequent printings if notice is given to the publishers.

Possessions

These are just a very few of the possessions on display in the museum at Auschwitz in Poland. They show that the Nazis killed men and women, young and old. These items were found in the Auschwitz-Birkenau camp. There were 30 warehouses, crammed full. The Nazis tried to destroy these warehouses and the **gas chambers**, when they heard the advancing Russian soldiers were close to the camp. They left it too late to destroy everything.

Were there other victims of the Holocaust?

The Holocaust swept up thousands of non-Jewish victims, too. These included other peoples, such as Gypsies and Poles, that the Nazis saw as separate, 'inferior' races. The Nazis had definite, unreasonable ideas about race, as we shall see. People who did not fit the Nazi ideas about a perfect state were also victims – including the physically and mentally disabled, homosexuals and political opponents of the Nazis.

How do we know?

- One of the most important sources of information about the Holocaust is the memories of people who survived it.
- Many people who did not survive the Holocaust kept diaries and collected photographs and other evidence. Some of them managed to hide this evidence, or leave it with friends, so it has survived to be used as evidence today.
- The Nazis kept detailed records; these documents show what went on during the Holocaust. When they realized that the **Allies** were winning the war, the Nazis tried to destroy the evidence of the worst of their crimes. They only partly succeeded; a great deal of evidence survived.
- A few places that were used in the Holocaust are still standing. Terezin in the Czech Republic was used as a **ghetto**, where Jews were shut in and forced to live away from other communities. The Auschwitz-Birkenau prison camp, in Poland, has also survived.
- In 1945–46, many Nazis were tried at Nuremberg. The lawyers at the trials produced evidence from survivors, from members of the **SS** (soldiers who had run the camps) and from people who had worked for the SS in various camps.
- The Allied soldiers who **liberated** the camps recorded what they were like in words, on film and in pictures.

The Jewish people

Jews see themselves as a people with common **ancestors** that stretch back to Biblical times. They are united by their religion, Judaism, by a common language of prayer, Hebrew, and by a strong culture. These things bind Jewish people together, but have also made it easy for others to identify and isolate them.

Judaism

The religion of the Jewish people is Judaism. It teaches that there is one God, who has chosen the Jewish people to be special. God will look after them, but in return, they have to live life according to his commands. Jewish people follow the teachings of their holy writings – the Torah. These writings were recorded on scrolls, written in different lands and at different times.

The Torah is made up of the Five Books of Moses, which are also the first five books of the Old Testament of the Christian Bible. Other writings also overlap with books in the Christian Old Testament. There are scrolls recording the teaching of prophets, scrolls of later teachings and stories passed down orally at first, which were written down later. The Torah covers all aspects of life. It gives instructions about diet, dress and how to behave to other people, as well as religious instructions. Jews are expected to pray at home, as well as in synagogues (places of communal worship). So religion and everyday life are tightly bound together. The Torah is written in Hebrew, the language that unites all Jewish people, no matter where they live.

Family celebrations

Family worship is as important as worship in synagogues for Jewish people. Each week on the Sabbath, families light candles, drink wine, eat special bread called challah and thank God for his blessings. Holy days are also celebrated in the home. This Polish Jewish family, photographed in Lodz in the early 1930s, is celebrating the **Passover** festival.

Dietary customs

The Torah has rules about the kinds of food that Jewish people can eat and how it should be prepared. Jews can only eat certain kinds of meat; for instance, they cannot eat pigs or rabbits. The meat they do eat has to be prepared by butchers in a particular way. The need to buy the right kind of meat, butter, bread and so on. This was one reason why Jewish people chose to live together. This photo of a Jewish butcher's shop was taken in Danzig in Poland in the 1930s.

A sense of community

The Torah tells Jewish people to take care of others, especially the poor and the sick. It also values education, and children are taught to read Hebrew at an early age so they will be able to read the Torah. Jewish communities set up their own hospitals, schools and other institutions to care for the old, sick and orphaned.

Flung across the world

Historians tell how, in New Testament times, the Jews were thrown out of the Holy Land, their land in parts of modern-day Israel, Syria and the Lebanon. Jewish people have moved around the world, settling sometimes for many generations.

They see themselves as both Jewish and belonging to the country that they have settled in. The Torah tells people to 'seek the peace' of the place where they are living and pray for it.

Differences in faith

While Jewish people share many values and beliefs, they have not always agreed about how to live. Mostly, Jewish people have argued over how strictly they should stick to the rules in the Torah. Some Jews say the Torah is the exact word of God. It has to be obeyed in every way and cannot be changed. Other Jews believe that the Torah is the word of God interpreted by people. They believe that some of the commands in the Torah, while right for some generations, can become irrelevant. They think people have a right to decide how they follow some of the rules.

Anti-Semitism

The **Nazis** were anti-Semitic. **Anti-Semitism** is being **prejudiced** against **Jewish** people. Although the term was first used only in 1879, anti-Semitism had been around for thousands of years. The Book of Exodus, part of the Christian Bible and the Jewish Torah, tells how the Egyptian pharaohs persecuted the Jewish people.

Was anti-Semitism constant?

Anti-Semitism was not constant anywhere. It flared up, in different countries for different reasons at different times. However, many Jewish communities have existed in the same places for hundreds of years without experiencing anti-Semitism. For instance, between about AD 500 and AD 1000 there are very few recorded instances of anti-Semitism in Europe. After AD 1000 there was a long period of persecution in Europe, which died down by about 1600.

This persecution varied in intensity. Some parts of Europe were unaffected, especially remote agricultural areas.

Why were Jewish people persecuted?

Jews were persecuted for different religious and social reasons:

- *Religious reasons:* Christians blamed the Jews for crucifying Jesus Christ. Also, very few Jews were prepared to change their religion and become Christian. For this reason, they attracted hostility from Christians, which could flare up into expulsions, persecution and murder.
- *Social reasons:* Jews were often seen as 'strangers', no matter how they tried to fit into the countries they lived in. Their language, faith and culture made them different. So, when danger or disaster struck Jews were an easy target to blame. They were blamed for economic problems, epidemics of disease and even natural disasters like floods.

Burning Jews

This medieval engraving shows Jews being burned during an outbreak of persecution in Germany in the Middle Ages.

The first ghetto

The first Jewish ghetto was set up in Venice in 1516. All Jews had to move to one of the smaller islands. Christian soldiers guarded the only two bridges off this island. Space was limited, as the number of people living there rose they built up. Jews were allowed to leave the ghetto in the daytime, but they had to wear special caps and badges so that people would know they were Jewish. The number of jobs they were allowed to do was limited.

Persecuting Jewish people

How did people persecute the Jews? There were a variety of ways, all of which were used by the Nazis when they came to power.

- They made Jews live in **ghettos** – separate areas within a city. When countries set up ghettos, Jews were forced to live in them and could not live anywhere else. This was very different from Jews choosing to live together to be near synagogues, schools and shops.
- Between about AD 1000 and AD 1700, many European countries also passed laws that said that Jews had to wear special clothing, so they could be recognized easily.
- Some countries expelled the Jews who lived there; this happened in England in 1290 and in Spain in 1492. When the Jews were expelled from a country they all had to leave within a certain number of days, leaving many of their possessions behind. If they had not left by that time, they would be forced out or killed.
- Sometimes anti-Semitic feeling in an area or country grew so strong that people hunted down Jews and killed them. Generally, this happened in only some parts of a country. For example, in 1106 the people of York killed 150 English Jews. It could also happen all over a country. For example, over 100,000 Jews were killed in Russia between 1648 and 1656.

Hitler and the Nazi Party

The **Nazi** Party, led by Adolf Hitler, came to power in Germany in 1933 by winning more votes than any other political party in the national election. They had not always been so careful to obey the law.

Adolf Hitler

Adolf Hitler was born in Austria in 1889. He did badly at school and then went to Vienna, hoping to be accepted as an art student. He was told he did not have enough talent. Hitler then spent five years living in poverty in Vienna, trying to earn a living by painting and selling postcards. It was at this time, he said later, that he began to hate educated people, **Communists** and **Jews**. He began to think that they were in a conspiracy to keep him from the success he thought he should have.

In 1914 Hitler joined the German army and fought in the First World War (1914–18). He was given several medals for bravery. Germany's surrender in 1918, and the harsh Treaty of Versailles that ended the war, horrified him (*see below*).

Germany was not only beaten, it was also humiliated. Many people, even those who had fought Germany, felt the Treaty was too harsh. Hitler thought that the German government had been wrong to sign the Treaty of Versailles. He decided he would go into politics and lead Germany to a wonderful future.

The Treaty of Versailles

- The Treaty took away all the land that Germany had gained during the war.
- It took away some of Germany's richest land in Europe and all of its colonies abroad.
- It made Germany officially take the blame for causing the war. This had not happened in a peace treaty before.
- It ordered Germany to pay for repairs in countries badly damaged by the war.
- It forced Germany to reduce the size of its armed forces.

■	Territory lost by Germany to other countries
■	Territory lost by Germany to the League of Nations
	Area formerly Austria-Hungary
	Territory lost by Russia
	Demilitarized zone

'One leader'

From the beginning, Hitler made sure his picture was everywhere. Christabel Bielenberg, an Englishwoman living in Berlin, had a landlady whose son collected cards like this one:

> 'Hans believed that he had found the solution to all Germany's problems. Over cups of cocoa, with picture postcards of Hitler in many different poses on the walls around us, he told me why the Nazis were the only party that could save Germany from complete chaos. One of their slogans was "One leader, one nation, one people".'

Going into politics

Many other Germans felt betrayed by Germany's surrender. Several political parties sprang up to oppose the government that signed the Treaty of Versailles. In 1919 Hitler joined one of these, the German Democratic Workers' Party. Hitler agreed with its aims and thought it was small enough for him to take it over.

By 1920 Hitler was one of the small group that drew up the Twenty-Five Points, the programme that outlined the aims of the Party. By 1921 he was its leader and had renamed the party the *Nationalsozialistiche Deutsche Arbeiterpartei*: the National Socialist German Workers' Party – Nazis for short. The Nazis stressed their support for 'the workers' against people in Germany who were 'exploiting' them. They argued that ordinary people needed work and food, which the Nazis would provide if they ran Germany. They said that the existing government could do this, but instead it chose to plot against the German people with Jews, Marxists, Communists, the rich and 'intellectuals'.

Nazi aims

Nazi Party aims included:
- scrapping the Treaty of Versailles
- gaining land in which to settle all German-speaking people
- taking control of even more land for these people to expand into
- ensuring only people of German blood could be German citizens – this automatically excluded Jews
- allowing only German **citizens** to have rights in German lands
- the state (government) should have complete power, but should use it to care for German citizens
- non-German citizens should leave German lands
- German citizens should put the interest of the state before their own interests.

11

The Nazi state

Hitler was sent to prison after the Nazi attempt to take over in Bavaria. While there he wrote a book called *Mein Kampf* (My Struggle), outlining his aims for the Nazi Party. These expanded the Twenty-Five Points, aiming to create a German **Reich** (empire) with a single leader – Hitler. One of the first things the new Nazi state would do was to retake the land Germany lost in the Treaty of Versailles. It would then take more land. The German people needed more room to expand into. This idea of 'living space' (*Lebensraum*) was important to the Nazis and was used to justify their expansion across Europe. In *Mein Kampf* Hitler said:

> 'There are huge areas of unused land waiting to be used. Nature has not set this land aside for any particular nation or **race** – it belongs to those with the strength to take it. A state has a duty to make sure that its people have enough *Lebensraum*.'

Hitler's new plan

Hitler had tried to take over the government by force and had failed. So, in a letter sent to one of his followers while he was in prison, Hitler outlined a new plan:

> 'Instead of gaining power by armed revolt, we will have to enter the *Reichstag* [German parliament] and win seats from Catholics and Marxists. Outvoting them may take longer than outshooting them, but we will win a majority and then – Germany.'

Storm troopers

As soon as he became leader of the Nazis, Hitler set up a private army of 'storm troopers' (the **SA**). The SA were regularly involved in fighting, usually with opposing political groups, to try to stop them from campaigning against the Nazis. At first, Hitler hoped to use the SA to take over Germany by force. In 1923 the Nazis tried this in Munich, Bavaria. They tried to take over the Bavarian government, intending then to march on Berlin. The plot was crushed by the Bavarian state police.

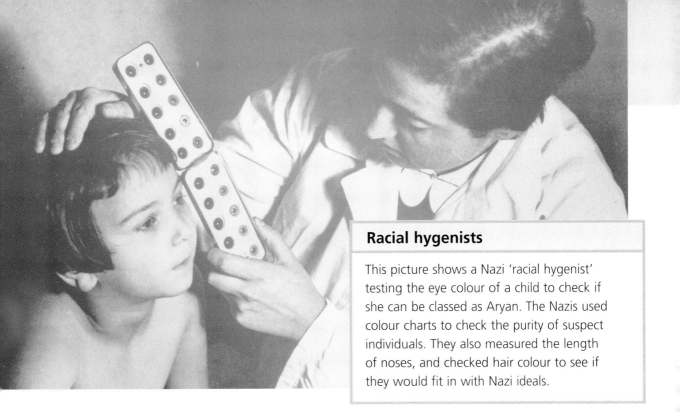

Racial hygenists

This picture shows a Nazi 'racial hygenist' testing the eye colour of a child to check if she can be classed as Aryan. The Nazis used colour charts to check the purity of suspect individuals. They also measured the length of noses, and checked hair colour to see if they would fit in with Nazi ideals.

Racial superiority

From about AD 1300, European explorers came across groups of people that did not look like them or behave like them. Differences in behaviour were put down mainly to physical differences, which were explained in terms of different **ancestors**. So, Europeans divided people up into different racial groups, depending on their ancestry. They assumed, wrongly, that Europeans were superior. In 1835 a Frenchman set out levels of superiority among white Europeans. He said: 'I believe that the *Aryan* race – white Europeans of the blonde, Nordic type – are superior.' The Nazis took this idea of superior Aryans and added the idea that these people all had 'pure German blood'. This made the nonsense worse. But the idea that Aryans were better was useful to the Nazis. It allowed them to excuse any mistreatment of non-Aryans.

Racial purity

Nazi ideas about an Aryan race that had 'pure German blood' were wrong. But Nazi scientists invented proof for it and it became one of the Nazis most important beliefs. Hitler said in *Mein Kampf*: 'No boy or girl must leave school without having a clear understanding of racial purity and the importance of keeping the racial blood pure.'

The Nazis also believed that German citizens should be healthy. The 'unfit' – physically or mentally disabled, or **asocials**, such as beggars and drunks – should be weeded out. They, like non-Aryans, could pollute pure German blood. Ideas about social groups were being discussed in other countries, too. In 1910 even the English politician Winston Churchill suggested in Parliament that about 100,000 'degenerate' British should have medical operations to stop them having children, or should be shut away.

13

Nazi rallies

While Hitler was in prison, the Nazi Party collapsed. As soon as he was released, in 1924, Hitler set up the Nazi Party again and began to work to take over Germany by winning votes in elections. He was a good speaker so he made sure that the Nazi campaign used lots of big meetings, called rallies, where he spoke. In that way, he got his ideas over to as many people as possible.

Hitler's speeches

Hitler's speeches all followed a carefully calculated pattern. They began with the history of Germany and the Nazi Party. Then came some information – often a government decision, such as introducing **rationing**. The reasons were given, mixed with angry accusations against people (such as Communists or Jews) that Hitler wanted Germans to hate. The speeches ended with Hitler telling the audience he would work hard to make Germany glorious and so must they. Hitler had a series of photos taken of himself making dramatic gestures, so he could decide which were the most effective ones to use in speechmaking. Stefan Lorant, a Hungarian journalist in Berlin in the 1930s, described the effect of Hitler's speeches:

> 'The audience was hypnotized. It shouted with joy; it yelled; it wept. The meeting had nothing to do with politics anymore. It had become a mass of believers in miracles.'

Propaganda

Hitler was very aware of the power of **propaganda**. Propaganda is information and ideas given to people in a way that will make them accept these ideas. From 1924 the Nazis used posters, radio broadcasts, leaflets, rallies and demonstrations to put over the points they wanted to make. They kept each message simple and repeated it over and over again. They used words like 'we' and 'our' that suggested that the Nazis and the voters were on the same side. By a carefully calculated use of violence against other political parties, and propaganda that stressed the rises in unemployment and cost of living under the government of the time, Hitler and the Nazis won 230 of the 615 seats in the *Reichstag* in the 1933 election.

Fixing opinion

The Nazis thought far enough ahead to make sure that the national radio announcer was changed for the election report. The new one was a Nazi, full of enthusiasm for Hitler:

'Like a blazing fire, the news spreads across Germany: Adolf Hitler is Chancellor of the Reich! A million hearts are aflame. A procession of thousands of blazing torches stream up the Wilhelmstrasse. Everywhere torches, torches, torches and cheering people! A hundred thousand voices shout joyously, *"Sieg Heil! Heil Hitler!"* into the night! The little old grandmother down there in the crowd says what they are all feeling: "Thank you, God, for letting us live to see this day!"'

Even if there had only been a few hundred people in the crowd, the radio broadcast fixed a picture in the minds of many people who heard it, all over the world, of wild joy at Hitler's victory.

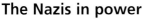

The Nazis in power

Once the Nazis came to power, they began by making sure they stayed there. In July 1933 they banned all other political parties. They set up the **Third Reich** led by the ***Führer*** (leader) Adolf Hitler. They began to wipe out all opposition. They set up **concentration camps** – prisons where anyone could be sent, without trial, for being 'a danger to the nation'. Most camp prisoners in the early 1930s were political opponents, especially Communists. The Nazis saw the Communists as dangerous because they had very different beliefs from the Nazis and because they had also been gaining support in Germany. They were, in some ways, the biggest political threat to the Nazis. Later, these concentration camps were used for people arrested on racial grounds – Poles, Russians and Jews.

An obedient nation

The Nazis had always said that no single person's rights were more important than the 'good' of Germany. They, of course, were convinced that they knew what was good for Germany. Their view was that to make Germany great they needed obedient citizens. So they expected 'good Germans' to put Germany first and obey the Nazis by, for example, accepting low wages, reporting a family member as disloyal to the Nazis or reporting a neighbour as a Communist.

Jews in Germany in the 1930s

When the **Nazis** came to power in 1933 there were about 503,000 **Jewish** people in Germany. This was less than one out of every hundred people – not many when the Nazis were saying that Germany was overrun with Jews. Many of them had been born in Germany, as had their parents and grandparents. They saw themselves as German. Many of their non-Jewish neighbours did, too. Many German Jews did not live or work separately from other Germans; they were part of the same community. Some Jews married non-Jews, either giving up their Jewish faith or converting the person they married to Judaism.

German businesses

Many German Jews ran their own small businesses, carefully built up over many years. As well as having their emotional roots, family and friends in Germany, they had all their savings tied up in Germany, too. They did not want to leave. Many believed Hitler was not against ordinary Jews who lived quietly. Bertha Leverton, a Jewish girl living in Munich, remembers:

> 'Unfortunately my parents thought: "The Nazis don't mean us. They just mean the rich Jews with the big firms and big, big, businesses. We'll stay put. It'll all blow over."'

A lot to leave

Artur Eisenstadt's clothing shop, Siegmund Eisenstadt, was inherited from his father and here photographed in the early 1930s. Artur chose not to leave Berlin, his home, his family and his business. He was arrested in 1941 and died in Sachsenhausen camp the following year.

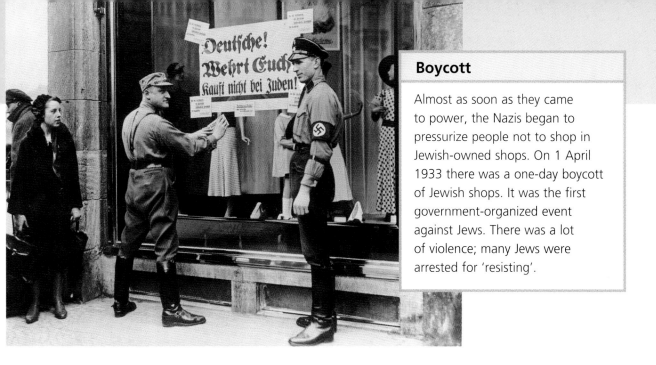

Anti-Semitism in action

As soon as they came to power, the Nazis began to put their racial theories into practice. They increased anti-Jewish **propaganda**. Nazi groups, such as the **Hitler Youth** and the **SA**, used violence against Jews and encouraged ordinary people to do this, too. The Nazis heaped as many 'sins' as they could invent on the heads of the Jewish people. So they said that Jews had 'bad' blood, were **Communists**, caused Germany to lose the First World War and were making money at the expense of the German people. By the late 1930s Nazi accusations were wilder: Jews murdered Germans regularly, even sacrificed non-Jewish children in their religious ceremonies.

Legal persecution

The Nazis passed laws against the Jews, making living in Germany increasingly difficult. On 7 April 1933, Jewish government workers, including civil servants and teachers lost their jobs.

Next, Jews were banned from sport, 'cultural activities' and journalism. They could not join the army or go to university. Rules were made to make life difficult and humiliating for Jews. They had to use separate park benches and public transport. They could not use public swimming pools, keep pets or use 'Jewish names' in telegrams.

The Nuremberg Laws

As laws were enforced against Jews, it became clear that no one was sure what made a person legally Jewish. In 1935 the Nuremberg Laws declared what made a person Jewish in Nazi law: anyone with three Jewish grandparents, or two Jewish grandparents who followed the Jewish faith was Jewish, even if they had given up the Jewish faith. To the Nazis it was ancestry, not religion, that made a person Jewish. The Nuremberg Laws also said that Jews could not be German **citizens**, marry non-Jews or employ anyone under the age of 45 who was of 'German blood'.

Leaving Germany

Getting out early

We have seen how hard it was for some **Jewish** people to decide to leave Germany. Even so, people did leave. The Franks, a Jewish family living in Frankfurt, had considered leaving in 1932. They waited because, as Otto Frank explained:

> 'When we heard the **SA** singing songs like "When Jewish blood splatters off the knife ... " we talked of leaving. But there was the question: How will you support yourself if you go away and give up almost everything?'

They were able to leave in 1933 because Edith Frank's brother helped Otto to set up a business in Amsterdam, in the Netherlands.

By 1936 about 78,000 Jewish people, roughly one in six of the Jewish population in Germany in 1933, had left. Those who left usually had the fewest ties to Germany and had enough money to start life again somewhere else. Many of them went to nearby European countries, like France and the Netherlands.

Anne Frank

Once out of Germany, people settled down to build a new life in their new country. They could relax, even enjoy themselves. They had no way of knowing that the German army would march into country after country in mainland Europe. They thought they were safe. In the Netherlands, Otto and Edith Frank's two daughters, Anne and Margot, went to local schools in Amsterdam, learned Dutch and made lots of friends. This picture shows Anne, circled at the back, with her classmates at school.

Where to go?

People often, but not always, moved to countries where they already had family or friends. Families or friends could help arrange emigration and work. They could put them up when they first arrived, and their friends' friends became their friends. All this made it easier to settle. But there were other things to think about when deciding where to go. Most Jewish **refugees** went to other European countries. These countries were easier and cheaper to get to and many people felt it would be easier to settle into another country in Europe.

Some refugees wanted to leave Europe altogether. Many wanted to go to the USA. But they had to have a visa, and the USA gave out only a set number of visas to any country each year. Another destination was Palestine, run by the British since 1917.

Nazi policy

In the early 1930s, **Nazi** policy about Jewish emigration was not clear. Herman Goering, the Nazi in charge of Jewish emigration, had ordered that Jews should be encouraged to emigrate 'by all available means'. However, the Nazis heavily 'taxed' those who were leaving. This made it harder for them to take anything valuable out of the country. Many lost up to half of all their wealth on leaving. This made it more difficult to start a new life, so fewer wanted to go.

In 1936, during the Olympic Games when there were many more foreigners in Germany than usual, the Nazis were much less brutal to Jewish people. Some refugees even believed that the worst was over and returned to Germany. Many people left the decision to leave until it was too late. From 1938 it became increasingly difficult to leave the country.

Quotas

During the 1930s many countries had economic problems – unemployment, hunger and homelessness. Governments did not want to add to these problems by taking in large numbers of immigrants from other countries. The USA had a 'quota system' – only a set number of people could emigrate to the USA each year. Most other countries had immigration laws of some kind.

The Evian Conference

In July 1938, in the French town of Evian, 32 governments sent representatives to a meeting organized by the USA to discuss the refugees. By this time most countries had a quota system. They were concerned not to increase their economic and social problems and made few allowances for the desperate situation of German Jews. Most representatives refused to raise their country's quota.

Some said harsh, **anti-Semitic** things. Australia's representative said: 'We don't have a racial problem – and we don't want one', while Canada's said: 'None is too many', meaning they did not want to take in any Jewish refugees. The Netherlands and Denmark were the only European countries to raise their quotas slightly.

Some who helped

Many individuals, both Christians and Jews, all over the world, worked hard to bring in as many refugees as possible. Various committees, such as the US Committee for the Protection of European Children, raised money, found homes and so on. There were Jewish communities in most parts of the world, who worked to get refugees out of Germany and help them settle in their new homes. All these groups would have found their work much easier with government support.

Open mockery

By February 1939, when this photo was taken, blatant anti-Semitism was common in Germany. These actors are mocking Jews and Jewish ceremonies. The float in the background has a model of a burning synagogue on it.

NORWAY 2000
SWEDEN 3000
NETHERLANDS 30,000
CANADA 6000
GREAT BRITAIN 52,000
DENMARK 3000
BELGIUM 12,000
HUNGARY 3000
USA 102,200
FRANCE 30,000
YUGOSLAVIA 7000
JAPAN 300
PORTUGAL 10,000
SPAIN 3000
PALESTINE 33,400
SHANGHAI, CHINA 20,000
ITALY 5000
PHILIPPINES 700
VENEZUELA 600
SWITZERLAND 5000
BRAZIL 8000
SOUTH AFRICA 26,100
BOLIVIA 7000
AUSTRALIA 3500
CHILE 14,000
URUGUAY 2200
ARGENTINA 63,500

Scattering worldwide

This map shows where German Jews went from 1933 to the end of 1938.

The USA had helped German refugees at first. It had not increased its quota of people allowed in from Germany, but it gave out visas for several years in advance. So people could go to the USA in 1938 if they had a visa for 1940. But by 1939 all the USA visas for Germany for 1939, 1940 and 1941 had been given out. To go on giving out visas in advance would be like having no quotas at all. So the USA embassies in Germany were told that refugees on the 1942 quota could not enter the USA until that date. People were desperate to leave, but their chances of leaving were shrinking. The number of Jewish people committing suicide rose rapidly. The only place in the world Jewish refugees could go to without a visa was Shanghai in China – a one-way ticket allowed anyone to live there. The Jewish community already in Shanghai had to cope with huge numbers of refugees, most of them penniless.

The Nazis also sent ships full of refugees to Shanghai. They forced Jews to board and charged them for tickets. While the poor were forced into Shanghai, the rich could try other methods. Georg Landauer, Director of the Central Bureau for the Settlement of German Jews in Palestine, said that in 1939:

'Travel agencies, mainly in Paris, get in touch with embassies that can be bribed – mainly Central and Southern American republics – and buy visas at high prices. They then charge a high fee for getting these expensive visas.'

Once war broke out in Europe, on 3 September 1939, getting out of Germany became even harder. And as Germany began to take over other countries in Europe, Jewish people in these countries came under Nazi control again.

Frank Foley

Bribery was not the only way to bend the rules. Frank Foley, the British Passport Controller for emigration to Palestine, based in Berlin, helped many people to get away. The British controlled Palestine and set quotas in 1936. Foley said:

'We wish we could help as many people as we once did; we could get thousands out, not hundreds. Conditions are getting worse here for the Jews. I dread to think how they will suffer in the coming winter. They have no money, few ways of earning any and there is very little housing. The quota is a calamity.'

How did Foley help?

Foley did as much as he could. He accepted obviously false guarantees of money (needed to get into Palestine) and granted more visas than he was supposed to. When he could not get people to Palestine, he also helped them to get fake visas to South American countries. If all else failed, he knew a number of escape routes in Europe that they could use, although this was the most dangerous way to try to get out. Foley left Berlin in late August 1939. Hubert Pollack, a Jewish lawyer who worked with Foley, and who Foley helped to leave in 1939, said:

'The number of Jews saved from Germany would have been tens of thousands less, yes, tens of thousands less, if another official had sat in Foley's place and applied the rules strictly.'

Leaving Germany

This diagram shows the number of Jews leaving Germany from 1933 to 1945.

These official figures do not include the people who left by escape routes.

After war broke out in September 1939, borders were closed – even **Aryans** had difficulty leaving the country.

Year	Number
1933	38,000
1934	22,000
1935	21,000
1936	24,500
1937	23,500
1938	40,000
1939	78,000
1940	15,000
1941	8000
1942	None
1943	500
1944	None
1945	None

Sailing to safety?

On 13 May 1939, a group of 930 refugees set off from Hamburg in Germany to sail to the USA on the liner *St Louis*. Of these, 734 had USA visas for 1942. Once they reached the Caribbean, they tried to find countries to take them in until 1942. Almost all the South American countries refused. Only Cuba said it would take 24, no more. It even refused to take the families of people already living in Cuba, once it had got 24. The ship sailed on to anchor off Miami on the coast of Florida. The refugees sent a personal message to the President of the United States, F. D. Roosevelt, asking permission to enter. He refused because they had no visas. The *St Louis* had to return to Europe.

When the *St Louis* reached Antwerp in Belgium, the refugees were a big news story. Journalists and cameramen met them when they docked. The refugees made more appeals for countries to take them in.

Safe at last?

They all found homes outside Germany. Britain took 287. France, Belgium and the Netherlands took the remaining 619. But as Germany took over more and more of Europe, the refugees from the *St. Louis* were back under Nazi control. By the end of the war, about 600 of the refugees who had been forced to return to Europe were dead – murdered in the **Holocaust**.

Kristallnacht

Kristallnacht means 'The Night of Broken Glass'. It took place on 9 November 1938, when the **Nazis** organized an attack on synagogues and **Jewish** businesses and homes all over Germany.

The official motive

The Nazis said *Kristallnacht* was a response to the murder of a Nazi official in Paris by a young Jew on 7 November. Herschel Grynszpan shot a Nazi official from the German embassy in Paris. They said he did this because his parents were in a group of several hundred Polish Jews living in Germany who were rounded up, taken to the Polish border and dumped there. As news of the Nazi official's murder spread the next day, there was some violence against Jews in particularly **anti-Semitic** parts of Germany, such as Hesse. The Nazis encouraged this, while saying they were only involved in the violence to try to stop it.

Careful planning

In fact, official Nazi documents show that *Kristallnacht* was carefully planned as a countrywide action. The Nazis had just been waiting for an incident to use as an excuse for the attacks. Overnight about 200 synagogues were destroyed across Germany and, according to an official Nazi report, 'most' Jewish homes and businesses were damaged, if not destroyed. This level of destruction in such a short time could only have been possible with careful planning. The **Gestapo** in each area had already been told:

> 'As many Jews as possible, especially rich ones, must be arrested. For the time being it should only be healthy men, not too old. As soon as they have been arrested, they should be sent to the nearest **concentration camp** as soon as possible.'

Kristallnacht in Mosbach

A bonfire of the contents of a synagogue in Mosbach on 9 November 1938. Many people who describe *Kristallnacht* say that the Torah and other sacred things were destroyed by the **SA**, **Hitler Youth** and ordinary people.

The map shows locations in Germany and neighbouring countries:

THE NETHERLANDS

BELGIUM

FRANCE

Hamburg
Alexander Gordon

Berlin
Anne Fox

GERMANY

POLAND

Leipzig

Mosbach
Torah burned

Furth
Lorraine Allard

Regensburg

CZECHOSLOVAKIA

AUSTRIA

All over Germany

The *Kristallnacht* attacks took place all over Germany. This map shows the location of events mentioned in the text.

Kristallnacht across Germany

Ann Fox was a twelve-year old Jewish girl, living with her parents in Berlin:

> 'It began with loud banging and the sound of broken glass. Downstairs the Nazis smashed the printing machines in the corner store. My parents locked and bolted our heavy front door. Two sisters from a shop across the street came to us in their nightclothes, terrified.'

Lorraine Allard was fourteen and living with her parents in Furth, Bavaria. She had already experienced a lot of anti-Semitic abuse, but *Kristallnacht* was still a shock:

> 'I was woken at two in the morning by a terrible banging on the door. Two uniformed Nazis were shouting "You're all under arrest. Dress and come with us." We were herded to a big square. There were thousands of other Jews, thousands. They were beating up the rabbi. They had fetched the Torahs out of the synagogue and I think they were trampling on them. We were taken to a theatre and made to watch while they made man after man jump over chairs and whipped them when they fell. All men under the age of sixty were then taken off to Dachau concentration camp.'

Alexander Gordon, aged sixteen, was living in a Jewish orphanage in Hamburg:

> 'At 11 p.m. bullets were shot through the windows, there was all kinds of noise. We all went into the fields behind our building and hid between the rows of asparagus. Twenty of us sat there all night in the cold, we didn't know what to do. When one of us called the police, they just laughed. At dawn we went back to the house. The windows were smashed and everything was messed up. One of the attackers had waited for us. He said "Make sure you're all gone by this afternoon. Out! If not, can you see that tree? We'll hang you all on it."'

25

Nazi reactions to *Kristallnacht*

The Nazis saw *Kristallnacht* as a great success. Joseph Goebbels, in charge of Nazi **propaganda**, wrote in his diary:

> 'From all over the **Reich** information is flooding in: 50, 70 synagogues are burning. The ***Führer*** has ordered that 20–30,000 Jews be arrested. Now popular anger rages. It should be allowed to go on.'

Over 260 synagogues were destroyed. Many more were damaged. Jewish homes and businesses were looted. Some people were turned out of their homes so non-Jewish people could live in them. The Gestapo arrested 20,000 Jews and took them to Dachau, Buchenwald and Sachsenhausen concentration camps. The Nazis also set a 'special tax' on Jews for repairs – a billion marks. Of course, the money was not used to repair Jewish property.

Other reactions to *Kristallnacht*

Non-Jewish Germans reacted in various ways. Some of them were overjoyed. Carlton Greene, a British journalist in Berlin, wrote home to the *Daily Telegraph*:

> 'Racial hatred and hysteria seemed to take hold of otherwise perfectly decent people. Respectable mothers held up their babies to see the "fun". Non-Jewish women who told children off for looting Jewish toyshops were spat on and attacked by the mob as Jew-lovers.'

Not everyone was delighted by *Kristallnacht*. Bernt Englemann, who lived in Berlin, tried to stop the looting of Jewish homes in his apartment block. He remembers the next morning:

> 'We went downstairs. The landlady was already there. A carpenter was replacing the door. My mother asked him to look and see if there was anything else he could mend. "Sure," he replied. "I've already looked – it's a mess in there. What a disgrace. It makes you ashamed to be German." The landlady and my mother worked for over an hour, sweeping up the broken glass and splintered wood. Other women in the building joined in.'

Next morning

Jewish shopkeepers cleaning up after *Kristallnacht* on the morning of 10 November 1938.

Taken away

Jewish men being marched off to Dachau concentration camp from the German city of Regensburg, 10 November 1938.

Jewish reactions to *Kristallnacht*

Jewish people were shaken by *Kristallnacht*. They were especially shaken by the involvement of neighbours in the destruction and looting. It was no longer possible to believe that the Nazis were only going to persecute 'big business' Jews.

It was also much harder to believe that your neighbours would help and protect you from trouble. Norbert Wollheim remembers the crowd that watched his local synagogue in Berlin burning:

> 'The people standing with me in front of the burning synagogues may have felt ashamed, but they didn't dare say so. The Nazis had made it clear: they had concentration camps for people who spoke against them. There were some who made nasty remarks. They were glad it had happened. They said the Jews had got what they deserved. That really shocked me.'

After *Kristallnacht* many German Jews decided to leave, even if it meant leaving most of their possessions, even some members of their family, behind.

Herr Kahn, arrested during *Kristallnacht*, was taken to Buchenwald camp. Once released, he left Germany as soon as he could, using a local escape network. Camp conditions were appalling:

> 'There were about 6000 of us crowded into one barrack with no floor, just damp clay. We had plank beds, no mattresses, no blankets, no light. On the fourth day we were put into barracks with a bit more room. Those with money could buy food, eating utensils, clothes, medicine. We did not work, but had roll call morning and night, often lasting several hours. Many died just standing there. On the twentieth day I was one of about 300 to be released. We were shaved and our hair cut. An **SS** officer told us he hoped we had been rehabilitated and to prove it we should contribute to the **Winter Aid** charity. Then we had to pay for "tickets" home; no one could leave until all had tickets. We were warned not to talk about our experiences, or we would be brought back and never get out alive. "Processing" took all day, with no food.'

Hating Jews

One of the most important steps in the **Nazis**' persecution and destruction of the **Jewish** people was to stop other people seeing Jews as human beings. From the 1920s, they had produced a stream of **anti-Semitic propaganda**. They always talked about 'the Jew', which had a strange effect on many Germans. Non-Jewish Germans often believed anti-Semitic propaganda, even though they had Jewish friends and family. Bruno Hahnel was in the **SA** and said in a television interview in the 1990s:

> 'I had Jewish relatives. I was very close to two Jewish cousins, but this didn't stop me agreeing with anti-Jewish Party ideas and actions.'

'The Jew'

Nazi propaganda concentrated on making people hate the Nazi version of Jewish people: 'the Jew'. This imaginary person was working constantly against Germany and its people. Melita Maschmann was in the **Hitler Youth** and clearly remembers how the Nazis helped to make real Jewish people less human:

> 'We were brought up to see "the Jews" as wicked. When I said in meetings that Jews were the cause of all the misery of the world, or that Jewish blood was corrupting, I did not have to think of old Herr Lewy, or Rosel Cohen, real people I knew: I thought only of the bogeyman "the Jew". And when I heard that "the Jews" were being driven from their professions and homes and imprisoned in **ghettos**, I automatically thought around the fact that this could happen to old Lewy, too. It was only "the Jew" who was being persecuted and made harmless.'

GROSSE POLITISCHE SCHAU IM BIBLIOTHEKSBAU DES DEUTSCHEN MUSEUMS

Anti-Semitic propaganda

A poster advertising the anti-Semitic film *The Eternal Jew*. The Jew on the poster is the Nazi stereotype of a Jew: a dark, heavy-featured moneylender, making a profit out of 'good Germans'. The Nazis showed Jews as harsh employers (symbolized by the whip) who worked with the **Communists** (the Soviet Union, marked with a hammer and a sickle, under the man's arm). The Nazis expected the German people to hate 'the Jew' and many people did, without thinking clearly about it.

Isolation

The next step in Nazi persecution was to cut Jewish people off from everyone else. The less contact that people had with Jewish people, the less likely they were to see them as real people. So Germans would be more likely to accept Nazi propaganda. Also, Nazi persecution of the Jews would be easier to ignore. The Nazis decided to cut Jewish people off by forcing them into ghettos in Poland taken over by Germany in September 1939. Security Police Special Units were told to set up ghettos as a 'temporary solution' to the 'Jewish Problem'. These ghettos were set up in Polish cities that had good rail connections. The Special Units were told: 'Jewish congregations of over 500 members will be dissolved and moved to the ghettos.'

Ghettos were set up in the most run-down parts of the cities. They often had limited water and electricity supplies and were crowded, often with more than one family in one room.

The Nazis then filmed the ghettos, showing the Jews as 'dirty' and uncivilized – having made sure they had no choice but to appear this way. A Nazi official visited Warsaw and wrote:

> 'If there are any people left who still sympathize with the Jews they should come and look at a ghetto. Seeing the **race** lumped together, decaying and rotten to the core, will get rid of any sentiment.'

The power of language

The Nazis used language to make the Jews seem less than human. They used the words 'sub-human', 'vermin', 'filth', 'vile polluters', 'corruptors', 'lepers', 'a plague' and so on – never 'people'. By the time they came to kill Jewish people in large numbers, they were calling them 'cargo' or *stuecke* – which means 'pieces' and was usually used to talk about things made in factories.

Real life

This is a photo of two Jewish children at a summer camp in Sweden in the early 1900s. If you compare them to the Nazi propaganda about 'the Jew' and the poster on page 28 you can see how they failed to fit Nazi ideas at all. They are fair, healthy, clean, well dressed and they are children. They are clearly not a threat to anyone. They are just ordinary children.

National festivals

This photo shows a Nazi harvest festival in 1933. Hitler wanted to get rid of Christianity because he wanted people to be loyal only to the Nazi state, with him as leader. However, he knew that many Germans were genuinely religious, so he did not fight the churches openly at first. The Nazis offered an alternative to Christianity, making Easter, Christmas and other church festivals into 'national festivals'. They tried to build in more and more pagan ideas, like worshipping nature, not God.

Did the German churches help the Jews?

How did the various churches in Germany react to the Nazi persecution of the Jews? Many of the established Christian churches were happy to see a strong Nazi government that provided welfare for the poor and that was against Communism (which the churches also opposed). Church organizations did not openly criticize the way the Nazis treated Jews. However, there were a number of church members who bravely criticized Nazi **anti-Semitism**. They were sent to **concentration camps** or executed.

The Catholic Church

The German Catholic Church did not protest against Nazi anti-Semitism. In 1933 it made an agreement with Hitler that he would not attack the church if it did not get involved in politics. So the German Catholic Church did not speak out against Nazi anti-Semitic policies; it even let the Nazis use its records to decide if people were 'Jewish'.

Catholic groups in countries not controlled by the Nazis, such as Britain and the USA, protested and set up organizations to help **refugees**, especially 'non-**Aryan** Christians'. This group included people with Jewish **ancestors** who had converted to Christianity but were classified by the Nazis as Jewish.

How did ordinary Catholics feel? Some condemned the Nazis; others supported them. Emma Becker was a German Jew who married a Catholic and became one. Despite this, the Catholics at her church would not sit or kneel beside her, or let her sing in the church choir. Only the priest accepted her – so his congregation turned against him, too. When the Catholic priest Bernhard Lichtenberg of Berlin asked his congregation to pray for 'the poor, persecuted Jews', he was arrested and sent to Dachau concentration camp where he died.

The Protestant churches

There was no single Protestant church, but several different Protestant movements that did not always agree. These churches reacted to the Nazis differently. The German Christian Movement accepted Nazi beliefs, including anti-Semitism. The Nazis gave this church more support than any other, for its members were happy to hang Nazis swastikas in their churches and preach Nazi ideas. However, there were too many Protestant churches for the Nazis to control them all.

Another new group, the Confessing Church, was set up to oppose the German Christian Movement and its 'political' behaviour. They were persecuted by the **Gestapo** and many members were sent to concentration camps.

Ways of resisting

As with the German Catholic Church, it was most often individual people, rather than whole organizations, that spoke out against the Nazis. Pastor Martin Niemoller was arrested on 1 July 1937, after a sermon in which he said: 'No more are we ready to keep silent at man's command when God commands us to speak. We must obey God rather than man.'

However, some Protestant churches opposed the Nazis more openly, especially when their governments were doing so, too. The churches in Nazi-**occupied** Denmark and Norway, for example, protested against the **deportation** of their Jewish populations by the Nazis. The Bulgarian Church joined the rest of the country in direct action to save their Jewish population. Jehovah's Witnesses, who refused to say 'Heil Hitler' and would not serve in the army, were banned from state after state in Germany from 1933. They were treated as a political threat and put into concentration camps. Other Christian groups, like the Quakers, worked secretly to help Jews escape. They did not speak out openly against the Nazis, but worked to save as many lives as possible while seeming to be 'good Germans'.

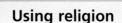

Using religion

While Hitler was certainly anti-Christian, he and the Nazis were willing to use religion to get people fighting. This army belt buckle bears the slogan 'God is with us'.

War!

War broke out in September 1939. By the end of October, the **Nazis** had set up their first ghetto in Poland. Jewish people had lost so many rights that they were finding it almost impossible to live in Germany – which was what the Nazis wanted. There were very few jobs Jews could do, and even those would be given to an Aryan rather than a Jew. They were being turned out of their homes, legally and illegally. Since *Kristallnacht* there had been more violence against Jews. Jews were also being sent to concentration camps, where many died from disease or the brutal living conditions.

Benefiting from Nazi policies

Were the German people against the Jews? Different Germans reacted in different ways. Many did not dare to argue with the Nazis, for fear of the concentration camps.

Others took advantage of the fact that, under Nazi law, Jewish people lost their jobs and businesses and they took these over for themselves. Others went further, taking advantage of the fact that it was clear that people could persecute Jews and get away with it. They could steal from Jews, beat them up – even kill them – and the Gestapo would not care. A young doctor remembers happily accepting Nazi policies in 1933:

'I wasn't much interested in politics. But I wondered if Hitler coming to power might be good for me. So many people were complaining that Germany had too many doctors. With Hitler in power he would "eliminate" the Jewish competition, so we "Aryans" could have a profitable practice. Please, don't misunderstand! At home we had Jewish neighbours we got on well with; our family doctor was Jewish. I wasn't **prejudiced**!'

Jew Free

Many towns, such as the Austrian one in the picture, threw out all their Jewish people, making the town *Judenfrei* – Jew Free. They then put up banners saying 'Jews not welcome here' (as in the photo) or 'This town is Jew free'. Some places even changed their road signs to show their anti-Semitism. One such sign said: 'Careful! Sharp bend! Slow! Jews – 75 miles an hour!' As towns were 'cleansed' of Jews, so local people who were not Jewish took over their homes and businesses.

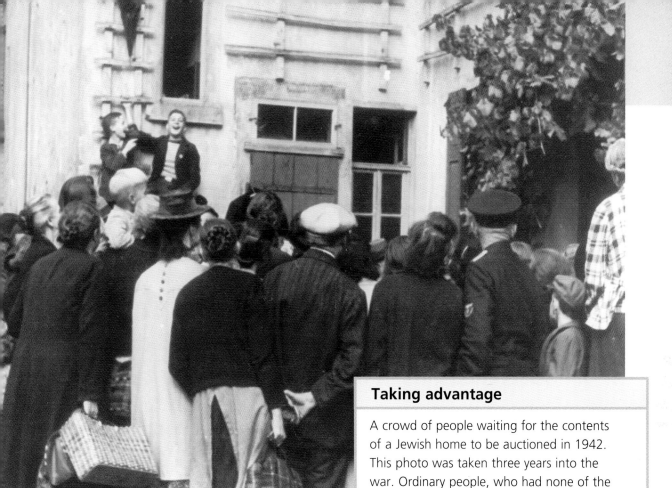

Businessmen

From 1937 the Nazis had 'Aryanized' Jewish businesses by taking them from their owners and giving them to Aryan businessmen. Sometimes the Aryan paid a small amount for the business, but never what it was worth. Many people were quick to take advantage of this. Others reacted against it. One Nazi party member and member of the SA had been given the job of organizing 'Aryanization' in Munich. He resigned, saying that while he was a good Party member and admirer of Hitler:

'I can no longer stand by and accept the way many "Aryan" businessmen are grabbing Jewish shops and factories at ridiculous prices. They are like vultures swarming down to feed on the Jewish carcass.'

One example of greed

Kurt Fuchel, who later escaped to Britain, remembers the day after *Kristallnacht* in Vienna:

'A woman had tried to buy our flat, but my parents had refused to sell. She came round the morning after *Kristallnacht* and said "It's mine now, don't argue or I'll have you sent to a concentration camp." She showed us a piece of paper with a swastika stamped on it. We had to leave. The woman had gone to the local government offices and had been given a document that gave her ownership of the flat.'

Legitimized killing

In March 1938 Germany had taken over Austria, which had never been part of Germany. Hitler said he was only putting right the unfair **Treaty of Versailles**, which had taken land from Germany. Then, in October 1938, Hitler, with British and French consent, took over the German-speaking part of Czechoslovakia (Sudentanland). On 9 March 1939, he invaded the rest of Czechoslovakia. Hitler had waited to see if the other European countries would go to war over Czechoslovakia. They did not. So, on 1 September 1939, Hitler's army invaded Poland. Britain and France then declared war on Germany on 3 September. But it was too late. The German army was too strong. It swept across Poland with stunning speed. Poland was divided between Germany and the Soviet Union, who, in 1939, had made an agreement not to fight each other. They also decided how to divide up Poland. Germany wanted the agreement because it did not want to have to fight in both the Soviet Union and Britain and France. The Soviet Union wanted the agreement because its army was not yet strong enough to take on the German army.

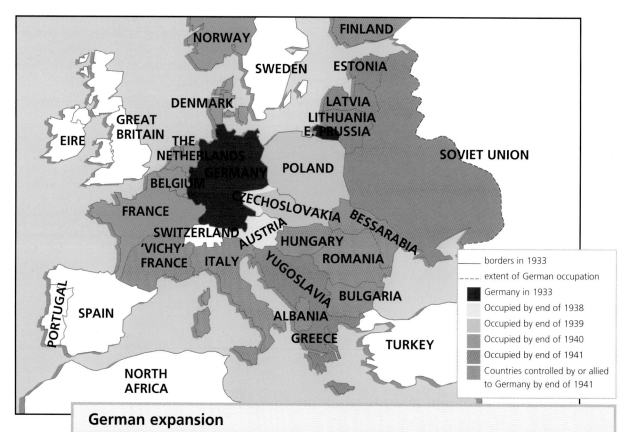

Legend:

— borders in 1933
---- extent of German occupation
■ Germany in 1933
Occupied by end of 1938
Occupied by end of 1939
Occupied by end of 1940
Occupied by end of 1941
Countries controlled by or allied to Germany by end of 1941

German expansion

This map shows how Nazi Germany took over more and more of Europe from 1933 to 1945. As the Nazis controlled more territory, more **Jewish** people were caught up in the **Holocaust**. In the early 1930s, many Jews left Germany for the safety of France, the Netherlands or Belgium, only to find these countries taken over by Germany during the war.

Mass graves

An *Einsatzgruppen* in action. Their system was to get a mass grave dug and assemble all the Jews in one place, such as the town square. The Jews were then taken off in batches, men first, then women and children. Everyone had to strip and then they were shot on the edge of the mass grave.

Not just fighting

The war changed German attitudes to non-**Aryans**, especially Jews. Hitler did not need to worry about what other countries thought of his actions anymore – he was at war already. Also, in war people get killed, so it is easier to blur the line between people who are enemies and people who are just 'rubbish', as the **Nazis** put it. So the army that marched into Poland didn't just pass laws against Jews and Poles (Poles were Slavs and so 'sub-human' to the Nazis). It killed them, too – thousands of them. It was in Poland that the Nazis set up the biggest **ghettos**, many **concentration camps** and labour camps, and the only **death camps**.

Mass murder

During the very first days of the war, Private Georg Neuber, a soldier in the German army, witnessed the cruelty of German **SS** and 'special operations units' towards the Polish people. Near Naklo, his company saw about 80 Jews murdered. In a village near Bromberg they found the bodies of over 50 Poles in a schoolhouse.

Not one seemed over 20; all had been shot in the neck. Soldiers from his company were not made to take part in the mass executions, but in the following weeks they had to watch many more. Time and again, Jewish men, women, even children, were hauled away and 'liquidated', allegedly for sniping. The same fate befell many Poles.

On 22 June 1941, the Germans invaded the Soviet Union, despite the Nazi-Soviet Pact. The Soviets were both **Communists** and Slavs – two reasons for Hitler to hate them. The invasion of Poland had been brutal. The invasion of the Soviet Union was worse. For the first time, the Nazis set up special murder squads, called *Einsatzgruppen*, that moved in with the invading army. Their official orders were to murder 'partisans' – local people who resisted the German occupation. It soon became clear that they were really to kill all Jews. The *Einsatzgruppen* used local people to pick out the Jews. These people were rewarded with their choice of the property of the dead.

Hiding the truth

The Nazis were killing Jews in large numbers, but they were still not openly saying so. They were supposedly 'executing partisans'. However, they were admitting to themselves that they now wanted to make German lands **Judenfrei** by murder, although they seldom talked of 'murdering Jews'. Instead, even in official reports, they talked about soldiers in the Soviet Union 'making sure the Jewish sub-humans pay a severe, but fair, price for their misdeeds.' When they talked of bad conditions in labour gangs and camps, they said these would 'naturally reduce Jewish numbers'.

Too upsetting?

The *Einsatzgruppen* killed thousands of Jews in the Soviet Union – in Babi Yar near Kiev, 33,000 people were murdered in two days. But the head of the SS, Heinrich Himmler, was worried about the effect of this 'work' on his squads. Himmler wanted less 'personal' ways of killing:

> 'For shootings you need people to do the shooting and it has a bad effect on them. It would be better to liquidate people using 'gas-vans' which have been made to my design in Germany. They remove the unpleasantness connected with execution by shooting.'

Recording a massacre

Einsatzgruppen in Dubossary in the Soviet Union on 14 September 1941. Two thousand Jews were killed there. Some squads had several soldiers firing into the mass grave. It was seen as 'less upsetting' than individual shootings, where a soldier knew exactly who he had killed.

Gassing in Auschwitz

On 3 September 1941, about 600 Soviet prisoners of war and 250 patients from the camp hospital were driven into a sealed cellar. They were gassed with Zyklon B gas, which the camp had supplies of because it was used for killing lice on clothing and bedding. Although people did have to make the prisoners go into the cellar, and did have to throw the can of gas in, they killed a lot of people at one time, without having to hear them die. Thousands of cans of Zyklon B, as shown in the display in this picture, were found at Auschwitz when the war ended.

Gas vans

So the SS looked for less 'unpleasant' ways of mass murder. They settled on gassing as the best method. At first they tried 'gas vans', vans that pumped exhaust fumes into the back, where the people were, while the van was driven around. The designers experimented to get them working efficiently. One report said:

> 'The vans must be smaller and packed solid to shorten the operating time. The makers said this would put too much weight at the front. It does not, because the "goods" [the people inside] rush to the rear and are mostly there at the end of the operation.'

In July 1941, Hermann Goering, Hitler's second-in-command, told Himmler that Hitler had decided that the 'Final Solution' to the Jewish problem was to kill them all. While the *Einsatzgruppen* were doing this in Russia, Himmler was to look for places for death camps. They had to be in Poland and isolated – with a railway line nearby. He also had to find an efficient and impersonal way to commit mass murder.

The Chelmno gas vans

Chelmno camp was set up in December 1941 – the first death camp. This is where Himmler's gas-van experiments took place. The vans pumped carbon monoxide exhaust fumes into the sealed rear compartment. SS scientists found that a sixteen-kilometre (ten-mile) drive from the 'load point' to the burial trenches, at a speed of 32 kph (20 mph), was long enough to kill the 'goods'. The gas vans were still 'too personal', however. The drivers often drove faster than 32 kph (20 mph), to get their job over. So the Jews were not dead on arrival, and the drivers had to drive around for longer, or the officers in charge had to shoot the dying people.

The 'Final Solution'

On 20 January 1942, the Nazis staged a conference in Wannsee, just outside Berlin. Reinhard Heydrich, head of the German security operations, called the meeting. The purpose was to plan the outline of the 'Final Solution' and to establish the authority of the SS in carrying it out. The camps and ghettos were overflowing, despite the appalling death rate from starvation, disease and the living and working conditions. 'There are about 3.5 million Jews in my territory,' said Hans Frank, the Nazi Governor-General of **Occupied** Poland. 'We cannot shoot them all, we cannot poison them all. We have to find ways to wipe them all out.'

The Nazis left the conference with two different aims. They wanted to kill all Jews in the land they controlled. They also wanted more soldiers, so they had to make workers join the army.

The workers who joined the army had to be replaced. Concentration camp prisoners could be worked hard and not paid. The Nazis set up death camps to 'deal with' Jews. These were mainly separate from the concentration camps and labour camps that provided workers.

Ready for mass murder

Jews from the ghettos, the camps and occupied Europe were taken to the death camps. Any Jews left alive were simply waiting their turn. Belzec, Chelmno, Treblinka and Sobibor death camps were built. Majdanek and Auschwitz had death camps added to the camps already there. In all the death camps, Jews were gassed in large numbers. From 1942 the SS in the camps and ghettos treated Jews even more badly. They were worked to death, starved to death, beaten to death and shot.

Ways of killing

These Jewish people are being transported to Chelmno death camp. They were told they were going to a different ghetto. While the death camps were working, Jews were still killed at random in the concentration camps and ghettos. Harry Balsam was twelve years old in 1942, living in the Polish ghetto of Gorlice. He remembers:

'Killing and shooting became a normal, everyday event. That is how it was. You got used to the idea that killing was nothing.'

Death camps

The death camps killed millions of Jews in just a few years. Treblinka camp was gassing people for a year and a week – 53 weeks. In that time it killed 700,000 people. This was 2000 people a day, every day of the week. By 1942 the Nazis had made Jewish people seem so unlike real people in some minds that they could kill them like this. Random violence against Jews from 1933, followed by more and more killings on a larger and larger scale, made killing Jews seem normal. The death camps ran a system that deliberately made the victims as unlike people as possible. This helped the SS who ran the camps to cope with their duty. The Hungarian journalist Gitta Sereny interviewed Franz Stangl, the camp commandant of Treblinka, in Dusseldorf prison in 1971. During the interview, it became clear that once the people undressed they had no longer been real to him.

Numbers of dead

This map shows the numbers of Jews murdered and the countries they came from.

A different way of looking

The following is part of Gitta Sereny's interview with Franz Stangl, commandant of Treblinka camp:

> [Gitta] 'There were so many children – did they ever make you think of your children?'
>
> [Franz Stangl] 'No, I can't say I ever thought that way. You see, I rarely saw them as individuals. It was always a huge mass. I sometimes stood on a wall and saw them in the "tube" [the fenced path to the gas chambers]. But – how can I explain it – they were naked, packed together, running, being driven with whips like ...' [The sentence trailed off.]
>
> [Gitta] 'Could you not have changed that? You were in charge. Could you not have stopped the nakedness, the whips, the horror of treating them like cattle?'
>
> [Franz Stangl] 'No, no, no. This was the system. It worked. And because it worked, it could not be changed.'
>
> [Gitta] 'What was the worst place in the camp for you?'
>
> [Franz Stangl] 'The undressing barrack.'

Reactions

How much did people in land **occupied** by the **Nazis** know about the **Holocaust**? How much did people in countries free from Nazi control know? There is much argument about this, even now. For a long time, 'ordinary' Germans claimed that they had no idea what was going on in Nazi camps, especially the **death camps**. Certainly, the Nazis did not publicize the death camps. This does not mean that people had no idea what was happening.

People must have seen the **concentration** and labour camps – many of them were based in or near cities. The author Daniel Jonah Goldhagen points out:

> 'Within Germany itself there was an enormous network of camps – it is not certain how many. If you count in the smallest sub-camps, Berlin had 645 camps just for forced labour.'

Making excuses?

Even today, there are people who want to excuse not only ordinary Germans, but also the **SS** and the *Einsatzgruppen*. One of the lawyers prosecuting people involved in the Holocaust said:

> 'So many people tell me they are "sick and tired about hearing lies about our soldiers", that the people we investigate "didn't know what they were doing" or "were just obeying orders". They knew. One hundred and thirty-two SS men in the Soviet Union killed 138,000 men, women and children in seven months by shooting each one in the back of the neck. They kept careful lists. How could they not know what they were doing?'

Far from invisible

During the war, concentration camp prisoners were used to clear the streets after British bombing raids. These prisoners are working in Bremen after the bombing raid of 13 June 1943. The Nazis were careful to choose prisoners who looked as well as possible, and they made sure they were reasonably dressed. In this way, they made camp conditions seem better than they were for many prisoners, especially **Jewish** prisoners.

Help at last

Rudolf Vrba (pictured right) and Alfred Wetzler escaped as the SS at Birkenau prepared to gas all the Hungarian Jews. Vrba remembers that it was clear what was going on:

'They were talking about "a million units", even "Hungarian salami". This had some effect – the British bombed the rail lines to Auschwitz, while the USA bombed Budapest, Hungary's capital city. The Hungarian government stopped sending Jews to Auschwitz. The escapees' information saved over 170,000 people.'

MINISTERSTVO NÁRODNEJ OBRANY

Čj. 15550/34/Vr-50   Kleg. 5. oddel. 1946

Vlastnoručný podpis majiteľa

We will never know how much 'ordinary people' knew and how much they chose to ignore. Some Germans refused to see the problems with Nazi rule. Many others lost their first enthusiasm for the Nazis, but felt powerless to change things. Grete Kulle, who lived in Berlin, remembers:

'My mother meant it when she said: "The riffraff have to be cleared off the streets. They will be re-educated to do honest work in the camps. They will be taught discipline and cleanliness, but will not be harmed." But you could not claim that you had no idea what was going on, not if you read the paper. People would say "Hush! Watch Out! You don't want to end up in a concentration camp!"'

Tomi Ungerer says the same thing about life in occupied France:

'The word "concentration camp" was used in posters as a threat. Stories went around that the wartime soap was made from Jewish victims.'

What about other countries?

From 1933 it was clear to people outside Germany that concentration camps were harsh, especially on Jews. During the war, the British heard of Birkenau almost from the very beginning. In October 1943, there were even newspaper headlines such as 'Hitler Murdered Three Million Jews in Europe'. But the British and American governments were focused on winning the war. Then, in 1944, Rudolf Vrba and Alfred Wetzler escaped from Auschwitz and said what was going on in Birkenau. Their report was widely publicized. It was no longer possible to ignore the facts.

Resettlement

Jews from occupied western Europe were first of all collected in **transit camps** in their own countries. From here they were moved to **ghettos** or death camps. This photo shows Dutch Jews being loaded on to a train at the Dutch transit camp at Westerbork. When people asked where they were being taken, they were always told they would be 'resettled in the east'. If they asked more, they were sometimes told they were being sent to new camps, or to farming areas in the east, even to a new 'Jewish State'.

Collaboration

At the end of the war, many countries and people were accused of 'collaborating' with the Nazis. This means they helped them and worked with them. Some of them collaborated willingly, because they agreed with Nazi ideas or benefited in some way. Others were forced to collaborate, by threats to themselves or their families.

Collaborating countries

Countries collaborated with the Nazis in various ways. Hungary, Bulgaria and Romania worked with the Nazis in return for not being invaded by Germany. They still ran their own countries, but they had to follow Nazi policies. They collaborated by sending their Jewish residents to camps in Germany and Poland. Occupied countries, which were taken over by the Nazis, collaborated in this way, too.

Did everyone collaborate?

It was possible to avoid collaborating, even if the German army was occupying your country. For example, the Danish people hid their Jews from Nazi officials, who only managed to find 500 Jews to **transport**. In contrast, France sent 77,000 Jewish people to their deaths, most of them rounded up by the French police, not the **Gestapo** or SS.

Hungary began by sending transport after transport of Jews – about 437,000 people. On the other hand, as soon as the USA bombed Budapest, the Hungarian capital, and demanded that the transports stop, the Hungarian government did stop them. They refused to collaborate any more and 170,000 people were saved.

German collaborators

People as well as countries collaborated with the Nazis. In Germany, people collaborated by reporting on and beating up **Communists** and Jews, throwing Jews out of their homes and so on. Some of the information as to where Jews and Communists were came from ordinary people, but the Nazis had a spy system, too. In 1936 a Nazi official wrote to a friend:

'Every staircase now has an informer who collects the **Winter Aid** contributions, gives out all sorts of forms, asks about family matters and tries to find out about everything under the sun. He talks to housewives about prices and food shortages, he pushes into people's homes to see what newspapers they read, how they live and so on. Even old Party members have protested about this snooping. Every tenant is visited at least once a week by one of these block wardens. They send in regular reports to their Party office.'

In occupied countries, people gave information to the Germans about Communists, Jews, political opponents and partisans – people who secretly fought the Germans, by blowing up bridges and railway lines or sabotaging the Nazis in other ways. Collaborators in occupied countries made a huge difference – if the local police and people did not help, then it was far harder for the Nazis to make lists of the Jews and act against them. Sometimes people were forced to collaborate. The Nazis were ruthless about threatening that people or their families would be sent to concentration camps if they did not help.

Punishing collaborators

Once the Germans were driven out of France, many people who had collaborated with them were shot or hung by local partisans. People who had run cafes the Germans used, or women who had had relationships with German soldiers, were also collaborators. While some people who were punished had certainly helped the Nazis and caused many deaths, others were killed in a settling of local rivalries. This photo was taken in Chartres in France on 18 August 1944, shortly after the **Allies** drove the Germans out of the town. The women had had their heads shaved because they had relationships with German soldiers.

Getting the children out

The **Nazis** were very clear about the importance of children. They began to teach Nazi beliefs before children were even able to walk or talk, using nursery rhymes that praised Hitler, picture books and so on. They also saw how important children were for the **races** they hated – they were hope for the future. So they saw wiping out the children of **Jews**, Poles and Slavs as important. Other people thought it was just as important to save these children, for the same reason. Rabbi Joseph Cahaneman put it this way: 'A child is an orphan when he has no parents. A nation is an orphan when it has no children.' When Jewish people trying to leave

Germany could not get permission for everyone to leave, or visas for everyone to enter a country, they often sent their children first. It was a hard choice, but many people made it.

Organizations worked hard in Germany and Britain to make sure many children got out in special groups known as *Kindertransports.* In September 1935, Albert and Paula Rabow were thrown out of their home in Koenigsberg. They decided they had to get 16-year-old Miriam out. The waiting lists for Palestine were very long, so they travelled to Berlin to ask Frank Foley for help. He got Miriam out to Palestine in about a month.

Hedy Epstein's family tried to emigrate to the USA. Their quota number came up before they had all the documents that they needed to be allowed to leave Germany ready, so they had to re-register and start again. They also tried Cuba and Lima, Peru. In the end they managed to get Hedy out on the *Kindertransports.* Her parents were sent to Auschwitz camp and died before the end of the war.

Identification papers

The US Embassy in Marseilles, France gave this letter to a Jewish boy, Werner Goldsmidt. It meant he could go to the USA on the date arranged by the US Committee for the Protection of European Children, despite the fact that the French government had not yet given him a passport. Werner was twelve when he left for the USA.

The *Kindertransports*

After *Kristallnacht* (*see pages 24–27*), it was important to get as many Jews out of Germany as possible. The British government said it would take in about 10,000 Jewish children from three months to seventeen years with no visa, just an identity card. The children did need homes to go to – either families or hostels set up by charity organizations. This picture shows some children arriving in London from Vienna, Austria.

Smuggled out of Germany

Before the war began, some Jewish children were smuggled out of Germany on student exchanges. The Nazis allowed 'approved' students to go to places like Britain. Bernt Englemann, now a journalist, went on several exchanges. Before his second exchange, Herr Desch, a local tailor, seemingly a Nazi supporter, spoke to him:

'Herr Desch asked about my school exchange to England – who organized it, how many were going, what the route was and how much attention the border guards paid to this regular group. When I caught the train, Herr Desch joined it with a party of sixteen children. When the exchange students for Liege in France left the train, Herr Desch's group did, too. One of the teachers told me they were going to the USA.'

By August 1939, Desch had got several hundred people out of Germany, most of them Jewish children. He gave them money and made sure they were safe with relatives or with his Quaker friends.

An humane official

Norbert Wollheim was 25 when he began to organize the *Kindertransports* from Berlin. He and the other supervising adults had to promise to return to Berlin or the *Kindertransports* would stop. He remembers one *Kindertransport* in particular:

'We were on the boat before we found that one boy was eighteen. I went to find him and saw his head was shaved – he'd been in a **concentration camp**. To send him back to Germany would be to send him to his death. We decided to say he was really seventeen. We landed at Harwich, dead tired, and I was called to the supervisor about the boy's age. I said he was seventeen in our records. We called the boy in to say when he was born (we'd made him learn the wrong year on the boat). He stuttered it out. The immigration officer looked at him shaking, with his shaven head. We were lying, and he knew we were lying, but he stamped "Admit" on the boy's papers and saved his life.'

Settling in

The *Kindertransports* saved lives, but the children had very different experiences in Britain. This partly depended on their ages, and partly on where they were sent to live. Some went to live with relatives. Some went to life with strangers, but settled in and had a fairly stable life throughout the war. Others could not settle and were moved from family to family. Most of the *kinder* left Germany expecting to see their parents again. Very few of them did.

Anne Fox

Anne Fox was born in Berlin in 1926. In 1933 her father had his job in a bank taken away and it took several months for him to find a poorly paid job in a Jewish firm. As the situation for Jews in Berlin got worse, Anne's Uncle Walter, who lived in London,

managed to get Anne's brother, Günter, a student visa to England. After *Kristallnacht*, Günter found a family to support Anne in England. Anne's parents arranged for her to leave. Anne remembers:

'The children met at the railway station, tagged and labelled, dragging rucksacks, suitcases, dolls, stuffed animals and musical instruments. Parents hid their grief as best they could. There were hugs and kisses, handkerchiefs waving from open windows.'

When Anne reached London, Günter took her to stay with their Uncle Walter. After about a week, Anne went to live with the Pincus family. Anne tried to fit in:

'Mrs Pincus was kind, but she was not my mother and her home was not our Berlin flat, either. I spoke some English, so was able to get on a bit at school. There was another German **refugee** in my class, called Mia. We talked German together, gossiped about our foster families and laughed at the strange behaviour of the British. We were a bit of a mystery to our classmates.'

How old?

This photo shows some of the older *kinder* arriving in Harwich in 1939. Parents tried to 'fix' their children's ages to get them on the *Kindertransport*.

Blitz!

In the late summer of 1939, the British government drew up plans for children and pregnant women to be evacuated from the cities they thought the Germans would bomb when war broke out. On 3 September 1939, the evacuation began. Although the bombing did not begin at once, when it came it was devastating. It was referred to as 'the Blitz'. This photo of a bombed London street was taken in 1940.

At war

The *kinder* arrived in a Britain preparing for war. This was especially noticeable for children, like Anne, living in London:

> 'By the autumn the British were imposing a complete blackout routine ... In school, we were told to be ready for evacuation. Everyone was given a gas mask in a cardboard box and we had to take a rucksack to school each day, in case we had to go.'

Anne and her school were evacuated out of London to Swineshead, a small village near Bedford. Anne went to live with the Manfield family, where she was very happy. At this time, she was still getting letters from her parents. By the time she was nearly 15, Anne was too old for the village school.

Günter found Anne a place at Bunce Court in Shropshire, a Jewish-run boarding school. In February 1941 Anne left Bunce Court, where there were many other *kinder*. While Anne was in Bunce Court, the letters from her parents stopped arriving. Günter had joined the army and, in 1942, he married a British girl.

In the summer of 1943, Anne left school and went to live with her sister-in-law, Constance, in Cardiff. She worked as a dressmaker's assistant and then at the local library. It was while she was working here, just after the war in Europe had ended, that she met a US soldier, Frank Fox. They became friends, married and went to live in Philadelphia, USA.

Kurt Fuchel

Kurt Fuchel was an only child, born in 1931 in Vienna. He and his parents were forced out of their flat on *Kristallnacht* by an '**Aryan**' who wanted it. His parents could see that it was important to leave Germany as soon as possible and seized on the *Kindertransport* programme to get Kurt out. Kurt was put on a ship to Harwich and was taken in by a Jewish family. Percy and Miriam Cohen lived in Norwich and had a son, John, who was five. Kurt remembers being met at Harwich and taken to the Cohen's home:

'I was scared, but they bathed me, gave me clean clothes and we had a chicken dinner. I began to feel more at home. I was sent for English lessons, then to John's school, which was small and had kind teachers. At first, I cried for my parents, but Miriam comforted me.'

Kurt remembers trying to fit in:

'I really tried to please my foster parents. Suddenly having a brother was a shock, as an only child. I was jealous and would say to Miriam, "You don't love me as much as John." Then she would say, "I do." I was really worried, once I'd settled in, that I would be sent away. This happened quite a lot. One family took in a girl who was the same age as their daughter and the girls fought all the time – hair-pulling, screaming, fighting the lot. So she went. You would have thought us exiles would have got together a lot, spoke our language, talked about old times. But we avoided each other. I was terrified that if one of us did something wrong it would affect how people felt about the others.'

VIENNESE LADY, 39, well versed in all house duties, perfect cook, also kasher cuisine, first-class testimonials, seeks suitable post immediately.—Kindly reply to Minna Pilnei, Brno, Havlenova 13, Czecho-Slovakia.

BERLIN girl, 27, good English, thoroughly domesticated, fond of children, good cook, urgently requires post; references.—Koby, I, Lancaster Lodge, Lancaster-road, W.11.

EXPERIENCED Viennese Cook-general (still in Vienna) seeks post; good references.—Write, Szerin Schey, 31, Northfield-road, N.16.

FOR good Austrian-Jewish maids apply personally to Celia Shure Domestic Agency, 17a, The Promenade, Edgware. 'Phone: EDG. 1925.

Looking for work

Lore Segal found it hard to settle and was moved around from family to family, because she didn't seem happy enough or grateful enough. She had a heavy burden to carry. Her parents had asked her to find people willing to hire them as employees, and so guarantee them work in Britain. Many *kinder*, despite their youth, were expected to do this, to get their parents out of Germany. People without anyone to search for them had to rely on adverts like these. Lore eventually found work for her parents. She got them out of Germany. But they had to work as servants and it ruined her father's health.

Together again

These photos show Kurt Fuchel (*far left*) with Deborah Oppenheimer in 2000 at the world premier of *Into the Arms of Strangers*, the Oscar-winning documentary film that tells the story of English kinder.

The other photo (*below*), shows Kurt with his parents in Toulouse, France in 1949. By the time it was taken the family had been together for almost two years. While all three knew they were lucky to have survived, they still found it hard to get used to each other all over again after such a long time apart. The Cohens found the separation hard, too. Miriam remembers the day they handed Kurt over to his parents. 'It was very, very sad. He didn't want to go. He didn't know them any more.'

After the war in Europe was over, Kurt's parents got in touch with the Cohens. His parents had escaped to southern France and some kind people hid them through the war. Kurt can remember how he felt when he heard the news:

'I was told that I would have to go back to live with them. I think I was horrified by the idea. Uncle Percy persuaded them that I should finish my education in England until my exams when I was sixteen.

'In 1947 the Cohens took me to Paris to meet my parents. I saw them coming towards me and I felt this really strong emotion – I was happy, I remembered loving them. We went out to eat and there were the Cohens on one side and my parents on the other and I couldn't really speak German or French, so it was hard to talk to them. They had let go of a seven-year-old and got back a sixteen-year-old. It was very hard for all of us. I was lucky, most *kinder* never saw their parents again, but it was hard for all of us to adjust.'

Most of the children who escaped on the *Kindertransports* did not find their families again. After the war, they settled in different parts of the world. They did not quite know how to discuss their experiences. It was hard to call themselves 'survivors' when they had escaped Germany and the camps. Yet they had been torn away from their families and most of them had never seen their parents again. They had survived and they had to cope with feeling guilty about that, too. It was not until many years after the war that a member of the *Kindertransports* organized a reunion and the *kinder* talked about their experiences and shared their anger at being sent away, even to be safe.

Timeline

1933

30 January	Hitler comes to power in Germany
27 February	Fire breaks out at the *Reichstag*, the German Parliament. The **Nazis** blame the **Communists** and produce a Dutch Communist who confesses.
28 February	German President Hindenburg's decree 'For the Protection of the People and the State' allows for the creation of **concentration camps**. The Nazis persuaded Hindenburg to pass the decree to fight what they called the 'Communist threat' after the fire at the Reichstag.
5 March	New elections. Nazis win easily with intimidation.
1 April	**Jewish** shops in Berlin boycotted
7 April	Jewish government employees, including civil servants, teachers and professors, lose their jobs
24–5 April	People with Jewish names can no longer use them when sending telegrams. Jews excluded from all sporting organizations.
10 May	Burning of books written by Jews, 'degenerates', liberals and Nazi opponents
October	Jews not allowed to work in the media

1934

5 March	Jewish actors banned
7 June	Jewish students banned from taking exams

1935

15 September	Nuremberg Laws passed against German Jews

1936

	Jewish doctors and dentists cannot work in state hospitals. Jews cannot become judges, join the army or work in the book trade.

1937

	Jewish businesses '**Aryanized**'

1938

13 March	Germany takes over Austria
15 March	German army marches into Prague, Czechoslovakia
25 June	Jewish doctors cannot treat non-Jewish patients
30 September	Munich Agreement. Czechoslovakia is forced to give the Sudetenland to Germany.
9 November	*Kristallnacht*; synagogues burned, shops and homes looted

1939

15 March	Germany takes control of Czechoslovakia
1 September	Germany invades Poland. Immediate action against Polish Jews.
3 September	Britain and France declare war on Germany
28 September	Germany and the Soviet Union split Poland up between them

1940

9 April	Germany invades Denmark and Norway
30 April	Lodz **Ghetto** set up in Poland
10 May	Germany invades Belgium, France, Luxembourg and Holland

1941

6 April	Germany invades Yugoslavia and Greece
22 June	Germany invades the Soviet Union; mass executions of Jews begins
1 September	All German Jews over the age of 6 have to wear a yellow Star of David with '*Jude*' in black on it
From September	Mass gassings at Auschwitz begin with Soviet POWs and continue. They focus on Jews and become more regular from January 1942.
10 October	Terezín Ghetto set up in Czechoslovakia; German and Czech Jews sent there
16 October	Mass **deportation** of Jews to the East begins
28 October	10,000 Jews selected and killed in Kovno Ghetto in Lithuania
7 December	Japan bombs US fleet at Pearl Harbor
8 December	First gassing of Jews at Chelmno, a camp in Poland
11 December	Germany declares war on USA

1942

20 January	Wannsee Conference; talks on 'Final Solution' to Jewish problem
21 January	United Partisan Organization, a Jewish resistance group, is set up in the Vilna Ghetto in Lithuania
17 March	First deportation of Jews to Belzec death camp in Poland
26 March	First deportation to Auschwitz concentration camp in Poland
27 March	First deportation of French Jews to Auschwitz
30 March–1 May	Bombing of German city of Cologne by **Allies**
15 July	First deportation of Dutch Jews to Auschwitz
22 July	Daily deportations to Treblinka camp in Poland from the Warsaw Ghetto begin

1943

18 January	Four days of unrest in Warsaw Ghetto over deportations
17 March	Bulgaria refuses to deport Jews
17 April	Hungary refuses to deport Jews
19 April	Warsaw Ghetto revolt begins
11 June	Himmler orders all remaining ghettos to be emptied

1944

23 March	Deportation of Greek Jews begins
7 April	Two Jews escape from Auschwitz and reach Brostalvia in Slovakia. News of the camp cannot now be ignored in the West.
15 May	Mass deportation and gassing of Hungarian Jews begins
From June	Death marches (called this because so many of the prisoners on the marches died while marching) from camps in Poland. Prisoners are marched westward, in front of advancing Soviet troops.
6 June	Allied troops land in Normandy, France
4 August	Anne Frank and her family arrested in Amsterdam

1945

17 January	Final death march from Auschwitz-Birkenau
27 January	Soviet troops reach Auschwitz
11 April	US troops reach Buchenwald camp
15 April	British troops reach Belsen camp
29 April	US troops reach Dachau camp
30 April	Hitler commits suicide
5 May	US troops reach Mauthausen camp
7 May	Germany surrenders
November	Nuremberg trials of Nazi war criminals begin

Glossary

Allies various countries that fought against Nazi Germany in the Second World War (1939–1945)

ancestors all the people in a family that have lived before the current members

anti-Semitism being prejudiced against Jewish people

Aryan used by the Nazis to mean people with northern European ancestors, without any ancestors from what they called 'inferior' races, such as Poles, Slavs or Jews. Aryans were usually blonde, blue-eyed and sturdy.

asocial the Nazis called people 'asocial' if they did not support the Nazi state. So they could be drunks, people who would not work, homosexuals or members of a religious group whose beliefs might make them oppose the Nazis.

citizen person who belongs to a country and who has rights in that country (such as protection by the law) and duties to that country (such as paying taxes)

Communist person who believes that a country should be governed by the people of that country for the good of everyone in it. They believe private property is wrong, including owning a home or a business. The state should own everything and run everything, giving the people the things they need.

concentration camp prison camp set up by the Nazis under a special law that meant that the prisoners were never tried and were never given a release date. The Nazis could put anyone in these camps, for any reason or none, for as long as they wanted.

death camp camp set up by the Nazis to murder as many people, most of them Jewish people, as quickly and cheaply as possible. The SS who ran the death camps mostly gassed their victims.

deportation being sent away from a place and not allowed to return

Einsatzgruppen (also called *Einsatzkommando*) special units of the German army set up by the Nazis. These units went into eastern Europe at the same time as the army. Their job was to round up and kill civilians who were a danger to the Reich. In fact, they were told to kill Jews.

Führer leader – the title given to Adolf Hitler as ruler of Germany

gas chamber large rooms, often disguised as showers, that the Nazis filled with people. When the rooms were full the Nazis pumped gas into them, to kill the people inside.

Gestapo secret police set up by the Nazis in 1933

ghetto area of a town or city, walled or fenced off from the rest of the city, where Jewish people were forced to live

Hitler Youth a Nazi organisation for boys, which trained boys to be fit and obedient to the Nazis. Boys were trained to become good soldiers. Girls had to join the girls' movement; this trained them to be good wives and mothers.

Holocaust means a huge destruction or sacrifice. It is now mostly used to describe the deliberate attempt by the Nazi government in Germany to destroy all the Jewish people in their power.

Jewish (Jews) someone who follows the Jewish faith. The Nazis also called people Jews if they had Jewish ancestors, even if they had changed their faith.

Judenfrei 'Jew Free' – a place with no Jewish people living there

liberated used to mean a place, especially a camp, being freed from the control of the SS. Camps were liberated by Allied soldiers.

Nazi member of the Nazi Party, which is short for *Nationalsozialistische Deutsche Arbeiterpartei*: the National Socialist German Workers' Party

occupied referring to places that have been taken over by people from another country and that are ruled by that country, often with an army to make them do as they are told

prejudiced being in favour of, or against, things or people before meeting or understanding them

propaganda information and ideas given to people in a way that will make them accept these ideas

race group of people with the same ancestors

rationing limiting the amount of a thing that any one person can have in a set period of time. For example, during the Second World War, food was rationed and people were only allowed a certain amount of bread, fat, meat and so on each week.

refugee someone fleeing the place they live, usually in fear of their lives

Reich means empire. *See* Third Reich.

SA short for *Sturmabteilung* – storm troopers. This was Hitler and the Nazis' first private army. Their violence helped the Nazis to win the 1933 election.

SS short for *Schutzstaffel* – security staff. The SS began as Hitler's personal guard. Later, they ran concentration camps and death camps. All the SS swore loyalty to Hitler, rather than Germany.

Third Reich means third empire. The Nazis saw their rule as the third German empire, with Hitler as the *Führer*, or leader.

transit camp a camp where people were imprisoned temporarily, before being sent somewhere else

transport used to refer to a trainload of people being sent to the camps

Winter Aid charity run by the Nazis to raise money to help the poor of Germany

Further reading

Auschwitz, Jane Shuter (Heinemann Library, 1999)
Diary of a Young Girl, Anne Frank (Penguin, 1997)
Ten Thousand Children: True stories Told by Children Who Escaped the Holocaust on the Kindertransport, Anne L Fox and Eva Abraham-Podietz (Behrman House, 1997)
The Beautiful Days of My Youth, Ana Novac (Henry Holt, 1992)
The Cap, or The Price of a Life, Roman Frister (Weidenfeld & Nicolson, 1999)
The Past is Myself, Christabel Bielenberg (Chatto and Windus, 1984)

Sources

The author and Publishers gratefully acknowledge the publications from which written sources in the book are drawn. In some cases the wording or sentence structure has been simplified to make the material appropriate for a school readership.

'The Nazis and the Church', in *Chronicle of 20th Century* (PBC Publishing, 1968) pp. 30–1
Anne Frank House, a Museum with a Story (Anne frank House, 2000) p. 18
Auschwitz Nazi Death Camp (Auschwitz-Birkenau State Museum, 1996) pp. 5
Auschwitz, Robert Jan van Pelt and Deborah Dwork (Yale University Press, 1996) p. 29
Backing Hitler, Robert Gellately (Oxford University Press, 2001) p. 33
Chasing Shadows, Hugo Gryn (Viking, 2000) p. 6
Foley, the Spy who saved 10,000 Jews, Michael Smith (Hodder and Stoughton, 1999) pp. 21, 26
Hitler's willing Executioners, Daniel Jonah Goldhagen (Abacus, 1996) p. 40
I was Hitler's Prisoner (yes, really), Stefan Lorant (Penguin, 1935) p. 14
In Hitler's Germany, Bernt Engelmann, translated by Krishna Winston (Methuen, 1988) pp. 15, 26, 27, 33, 41, 45
Into the Arms of Strangers, Mark Jonathan Harris and Deborah Oppenheimer, (Bloomsbury, 2000) pp. 4, 16, 25, 27, 33, 45, 48, 49
Mein Kampf, Adolf Hitler pp. 12, 13
My Heart in a Suitcase, Anne Fox (Vallentine Mitchell, 1996) pp. 25, 46–7
Nazism, 1919-1945, J. Noakes and G Pridham (University of Exeter Press, 1991) pp. 36, 38, 43
The Boys, Martin Gilbert (Weidenfeld and Nicholson, 1996) p. 38
The German Trauma, Gitta Sereny and Allen Lane (Penguin, 2001) pp. 39, 40
The Holocaust for Beginners, Haim Bresheeth, Stuart Hood and Litza Jansz (Icon books, 1994) p. 36
The Nazis, a Warning from History, Laurence Rees (BBC Books, 1997) pp. 14, 28
The Past is Myself, Christabel Bielenberg (Chatto and Windus, 1984) p. 11
Tomi: A Childhood Under the Nazis, Tomi Ungerer (Roberts Rinehart, 1998) p. 41

Places of interest and websites

Museums and exhibitions
Imperial War Museum
Lambeth Road, London SE16 6HZ
Tel: 020 7416 5320
Website: *http://www.iwm.org.uk*
The Imperial War Museum in London now has a permanent Holocaust exhibition.

London Jewish Museum
Raymond Burton House, 129-131 Albert Street, London NW1 7NB
Tel: 020 7284 1997
Website: *http://www.jewishmuseum.org.uk*
Or:
The Sternberg Centre, 80 East End Road, London N3 2SY
Tel: 020 8349 1143
The London Jewish Museum regularly features exhibitions and talks about the Holocaust.

Sydney Jewish Museum
146 Darlinghurst Road, Darlinghurst, NSW 2010
Tel: (02) 9360 7999
Website: *www.join.org.au/sydjmus/*
The Sydney Jewish Museum contains a permanent Holocaust exhibition, using survivors of the Holocaust as guides.

Websites
Before consulting any websites you need to know:

1 Almost all Holocaust websites have been designed for adult users. They can contain horrifying and upsetting information and pictures.
2 Some people wish to minimize the Holocaust, or even deny that it happened at all. Some of their websites pretend to be delivering unbiased facts and information. To be sure of getting accurate information it is always better to use an officially recognized site such as the ones listed below.

www.ushmm.org
This is the US Holocaust Memorial Museum site.

www.iwm.org.uk
The Imperial War Museum site. You can access Holocaust material from the main page.

www.holocaust-history.org
This is the Holocaust History Project site.

www.auschwitz.dk
The Holocaust: Crimes, Heroes and Villains site.

http://motlc.wiesenthal.com
The Museum of Tolerance's Multimedia Learning Centre site.

Index

SUPPORTING

EVERYCHILD